A L W A Y S
S U N S H I N E
Y E L L O W

PALMETTO
PUBLISHING

Charleston, SC
www.PalmettoPublishing.com

Always Sunshine Yellow
Copyright © 2023 by Anna Maria Gray

Illustration by EJ Woodke

All rights reserved

Paperback ISBN: 979-8-8229-1955-6
eBook ISBN: 979-8-8229-1956-3

ALWAYS SUNSHINE YELLOW

ANNA MARIA GRAY

Illustration by EJ Woodke

ACKNOWLEDGEMENTS

I would like to express my unending gratitude for my family and their support of my every endeavor. My grandmothers nurtured my love of reading and writing, believing in my dreams even before I was old enough to believe in myself. My parents and sister walk with me daily in this journey of life, despite the physical distance between us. Finally, Fred and my incredible children deserve gratitude and thanks for the daily love, inspiration, and support they provide.

Even more importantly, none of these cherished people would be in my life if it weren't for God, His perfect timing, and His boundless grace. To Him be all the glory.

WHY ALWAYS
SUNSHINE YELLOW?

As a little girl, my two favorite places to be were my grandparents' houses. My Grandmas, Sarah Anna and Celestine, encouraged me in my writing from a very early age, and I have precious memories of time spent with them and at their homes with cousins and my sister, Kendra.

Grandma Sarah Anna's and Papaw Gerald's house was almost magical to me; we had sassafras tea parties, we loaded canteens with water and set off into the woods behind their Rocky Top home, as we still affectionately call it, to embark on grand adventures; we were children, and children always seem to find the magic that is lost on adults.

The room in which we stayed on overnight visits was painted the most beautiful, vivid yellow, with plenty of windows, making the small space seem larger; evocative of sunshine, it was a perfect little world in which we played, recorded tapes of ourselves using funny voices, and dreamed up pretend scenarios that we acted out with the limitless imagination of children.

A few years passed, and as is its nature, time marched on at a pace that seemed faster with each birthday. My Grandma Sarah Anna grew weary with the colors of the house, and so our yellow bedroom was transformed into one with green ivy-patterned walls. It wasn't long after the change that she was diagnosed with cancer.

As she became more and more ill, I was testing the waters of writing poetry; I wrote a poem for her and for my Grandpa about being "over the hill and far away"; my favorite line reads: "Though the walls are green and covered with ivy, it will always be sunshine yellow in the corner of mind where stubborn happiness is kept." The yellow bedroom has become a symbol for me, a symbol of holding on tightly to childlike faith, and a reminder to savor experiences with the eyes of a child, with the eyes of that little girl I once was.

TABLE OF CONTENTS

LESSONS & RESILIENCE

LOVE & FAMILY

FAITH
& HOPE

TAPESTRY

you have taken joy into your own hands,
planted it mysteriously through my moments

like a tapestry of surprise,
i unfurl the perfect will you have for me.
empty me.
fill me up.
break me, and in your infinite wisdom,
create in me a new and more noble truth.

DEAR SHAME

You are no longer welcome here. Not now. Not ever again.

No longer will I hide myself away from a full existence to give you safe harbor.
No longer will I reside in darkness because of your insistence that I do not deserve the light.
No longer will I allow your voice to be the one that first reaches my consciousness, or your chains to hold me captive in a state of feeling comfortably numb.

I will not surrender to you even one more day of the life I was created to live. Too many I've allowed to pass by without participating because I feared that you were right. That I'm not enough. That I'm never going to be enough. That I can't possibly be worthy of love.

I will never again take you at your word, believing I am unworthy because of my many mistakes and missteps.

You came into my life disguised as a friend. When you spoke, it was easy to believe in you.

I believed what you said about God, about others, and mostly, about myself. I believed your warnings that no one could possibly love me if they truly knew me. You told me that I would never again be the person I once was and somehow convinced me that who I am today is "less than" earlier iterations of myself.

I see you clearly now, your evil motives, your cruelty, your jealousy. You used my greatest fears and insecurities to shake me, to ensure that I would learn to loathe myself enough to stay, enough to let your voice become mine. Your objective all along has been to steal me from myself. To make me forget who I am. And you succeeded for a time. You pushed and pushed, always in my ear, always whispering the lies you knew would hold me down.

Your objective was to silence me, to extinguish my self-love and sense of worthiness. To take my faith, my hope, and my joy. To rewrite my life through the lens of who you convinced me I was.

You took so much from me, yet I held on again and again, because your voice became familiar, became my truth. So convincing you were that I crumbled under your pressure. You said I wasn't enough; you said I never would be. You said I was a failure and a disappointment, a burden and undeserving of good.

You wrapped me in arms of false love, held me long enough that I became a stranger to myself. I no longer felt I deserved my life, my relationships, my kids, or even people I hadn't yet met. You pushed until I was paralyzed, unable to face day after day, until I finally began to wish I could disappear. For me, nothing in this life has been more painful than looking into mirrors and seeing a stranger reflected there.

But greater is my spirit and victorious is the God you tried to shadow, to make me forget. The flicker of a light within my chest remained. And grew. And built to a point where I could see the truth, illuminated. One day at a time, I have battled you since, chipping away at the walls you built to hem me in.

You, shame, brought nothing of any value. You almost took away all that I know and love. You crept in on quiet feet and methodically dismantled my life. But just as you saw it through as far as you could, I remained firm in my resolve to tear down the walls once and for all.

You wanted to end me, but you failed. Because of who and whose I am. I get to rise up again, my purpose intact, and as I follow you to the door, peace washes over me.

I'm closing the door. Shutting you out. You were the part of myself that hurt the most, but I have relented to the process of pulling your roots from the recesses of my heart.

You were only an illusion.

You are banished.
I am free.

DEBT

we are under the impression
that forgiveness is for the weak
or naïve
but let me tell you something:
offering an olive branch to
someone who has shredded your heart
takes a strength few possess
or put to action

ironically

when we forgive, it is we who are set free

FOR WALKS ALONE

thank you for walks alone
by water and brick-pillared gates
by pathways and open grassy land
for mothers and fathers and long distance calls
for rooms and naps
and long drives home
with music and singing
and flying fleeting thoughts
for Sundays and dinners and prayers
from Grandpa's trembling heart,
for your aching presence,
for the love that covers me

SEASONS

subtle whisper
of spring
a bird sings
a smell in the air
reminds me of flowers
and of home
though i am
weak and
weary
my God
speaks to me
with
gentle rain
and trembling
seasons

NOW

I used to believe the strongest thing I could do was hold on for dear life, but now I know that it takes just as much strength to know when it's time to let go.

I used to believe that I needed someone to make me happy, but now I know that the only person responsible for my happiness is me.

I used to believe that love was a feeling and a knowing, but now I know that it's an action, a daily choice, a promise.

I used to believe that I needed the approval of everyone around me, but now I know that the most important opinion of me is my own.

I used to believe that wisdom and wholeness were an endgame, an arrival, but now I know that growth is never linear, never finished.

I used to believe that I owed everyone around me an explanation for my choices, but now I know that I alone am authoring this life, that I alone must make this journey.

I used to believe I had to be perfect in order to deserve love, but now I know that perfection isn't real, and progress is what counts.

I used to believe success was measured by money and status, but now I know that nothing of this world has real value, and success is achieved in different ways by different people.

I used to believe that I was lost and had lost my purpose, but now I know that I'm exactly where I'm supposed to be for such a time as this.

I used to believe I would never do certain things, but now I know that we all make mistakes and we all need Jesus.

I used to believe I could trust anyone who called themselves a friend, but now I know that not everyone who claims they are trustworthy actually has my best interest at heart.

I used to believe that I could do or achieve anything, as long as I tried and hustled and planned hard enough, but now I know that only in Him can I truly achieve my purpose; all other ground is sinking sand.

EXCESS

Lord, pour yourself over me,
and allow the excess
to flow from my pen.

QUENCHED

the river of this life
rushes past my feet
so quickly that
i almost miss it;
as soon as i become oblivious to the current
and convince myself i am capable
of standing alone,
i am swept under, forced along.
when i surface, the water on my skin
cools the blaze of the sun
on my tender shoulders, and i am reminded
of His protecting touch.
He gives me floods to quench
the drought i can't even see.

D O

don't just learn;
experience, absorb, transform
advocate, prove, encourage
ponder, give, feel, do, listen
act, show.
live.

THANK YOU

the moon reflects a different light
and clouds are deeper
when i fall into this peace of heart

a shift in movement
in the echoes of my soul
gives me joy and a smile

your love is stronger than my anger
your blood can cover over even my darkest bitterness

thank you for the way your love attaches to a face,
a star,
a flower,
a dream,
and me.

TREE

I am a tree alone
new in Springtime bliss
looking all around for others like I am
soon, I find them, all alike,
and join their ranks

I am a tree alone
hot with Summer's sun
wishing for some space to be the way I am
but I can't find it;
trapped, I stand among the rest

I am a tree alone
crimson leaves unfurl
finding the blood of Autumn
that He has shed for me
allowing Him to change and shape, I reform myself again

I am a tree
Winter's death sets in
content, I do not search for worldly peace
instead, I bend my branches upward
and depart from this place

GRACE

alive
wanting
willing
curious

bending and moving—stretching

this body

i thought it was a shell
and nothing more
after everything changed
and I got stuck

but there it is—life—
blooming in my spirit
nonetheless

i guess this is grace
i guess it always has been

MY GOD

Creator
Sky Maker
Savior
Heart Healer
Open Door
Wooer of my Heart
Hound of Heaven
Almighty
Friend to the Brokenhearted
Great Mystery
Perfect One
Easer of Worries
Love of my Life

REMEMBER

when darkness settles in your heart,
when every step you take seems to lead you nowhere,
trust the One who brings Light—
the One who has sealed your future
and promises forever love, unconditional;
trust and faithfully serve where you are,
and when the time comes
for Him to lead you out of the pit,
follow Him
and live.

GIFTS

this moment
is God's gift to me
every breath a piece of the
grace-filled life He has granted
I am ever grateful for the moments
the chances to make much of Him
the re-dos and start-overs
made possible by the cross
I carry the Spirit
the gift of His own being
held in my imperfect—but fully loved—
human heart

PLEASE

please come to me and tell me
when I make you smile or laugh
please thank me when I help you
or set you back on track

talk to me each morning
if I held you in your sleep
share with me your lowest evening
and I'll hold you as you weep

just give me time each day
save a thought or two for me
don't you know I'd die for you
again on Calvary's tree?

B E

in this world of conflict
be peace
in this world of pain
be comfort
in this world of ugliness
create beauty
in this world of "me, me, me"
be like Jesus
in this world of duplicity
be who you were created to be

pray. console. help. love. do.

BECAUSE, GOD.

broken pieces
become
beautiful mosaics

dust
becomes
the filler that repairs the cracks in my heart

ashes
become
beauty

my mess
becomes
my message

my pain
becomes
my purpose

shattered hearts
become
whole again

because, God.

SEARCHING

I can search.
I can ponder.
I can plan, seek, wonder, and dream.
All these lofty verbs
I can put into action,
but nothing can fill the void in my heart
like giving silence a try and letting your Word manifest in me.

ALONE

I know you are there, and I trust that you love me.
You are my Creator and my only balance in a shifting world.

Yet, I am all alone, not because you want it to be so,
but because I'm too weak
to accept this weakness.

Surrender is all I need, and all I want,
and the only thing that makes me scared enough
to cry.

SOMETHING BIGGER

Something bigger
always comes
and sweeps away the lonely,
the empty, the sad,
and the hopeless.
Something sweeter
always fills
the void that follows
every heartbreak, disappointment,
and indescribable ache.

Something deeper
always cuts
the sorrow out
and makes new space
in an open, willing heart.
Something about
the Lord, my God,
cleanses away
all pain,
fills me again with laughter and joy.

I LOST MYSELF ALONG THE WAY

Somehow I lost my Self along life's way.
The only people who I thought could find Her were looking for their lost selves, too.

I knew She was in here somewhere, but I wasn't even sure if I wanted to find Her or hear Her voice. She had been my compass, the angel on my shoulder. And I had let Her down. I had rendered Her mute so that I could wander through places that weren't meant for me, so I could do things I never thought I would.

I'm learning that it's ok to be exactly who I am, if I can just discover who that is. I don't have to push or pull or bend or DO anything to gain that understanding; all those actions of trying to protect and control Her had just pushed Her deeper inside, until She was completely invisible.

Others would say to the version of me I created, "Its ok. I'm here for you; I'll always be here for you." And they could not fathom why I kept that wall, perfected that mask, skimmed the surface of life but no longer felt I was here to live it. I wanted them to see Her, love Her, protect Her, but I had hidden Her away, because I thought She was my weakness.

Little did I know that all my strength came from Her, that She had been vulnerable and therefore empathetic, that She had been confident because She knew to Whom She belonged.

It was through Her that God's light had shone.

She was no longer there when I looked into a mirror or the reflection in the eyes of my loved ones. She no longer had that light; I had too long left Her in darkness.

Me-Version-2.0 was just starting to give in, to give up, to stop the search and let Her go once and for all.

But just when I hit that rock bottom, and I knew that I could not continue on my own, I felt the hands of all those I needed most, holding me up even as I stumbled.

I resigned myself to the new me, the "after" version in the mirror, and I knelt in prayer with my shameful head bent low.

Nothing magical happened. I didn't get the answer I desperately wanted. But I made the decision to trust in God and to accept life without Her so that I could move forward from this place where I was held captive.

One day, as I was walking along, looking for God, I started to hear a familiar voice, and I started to pray more honestly, to trust that if I faithfully searched, He surely could be found.

I walked and walked, sometimes with a bounce in my step, sometimes with a pang in my heart for Who I had lost, and I knew God was not far away.

As I rounded the last corner, I knew I was almost there, that I would soon be in His arms, held as in the promises I had read my whole life.

As I drew nearer and nearer, I realized He wasn't alone. He was accompanied by someone I thought I knew, someone vaguely familiar. I ran into His arms when I realized with a jolt that it was Her.

"Where did you find Her, God?" I wept in relief. "Where has She been?"

He looked at me with all that love and He smiled as He answered. "It was not She who was lost, beloved Daughter; it was you. She has been here, with me, all along."

FINISHED

It is finished;
the tomb is empty.
Death has been defeated,
and life abundant awaits.

Retrace your steps,
your journey and your lessons,
and you will find evidence all around:
He lives!

God who empties graves:
may Springtime emerge as a promise,
a reassurance that you want to bless us much,
a reminder that what matters most
is never forgetting how much you love us.

CREATOR

in this compact airplane seat,
i am afforded a glimpse
of the Creator—
in the snowy ground
blending into the horizon,
and the map of towns
and cities down below

i can feel Him here,
feel the tug on my heart
to simply be still and
drink in everything He is and
all He has done
in my life

Creator, yes,
and Redeemer as well;
the revelation of this beauty
to my often unobservant eye
feels like a sign

it feels like Love and Joy and Peace
unlike i've ever known

it feels, finally, like i have come home

EN ROUTE

i met her on a plane;
where we were headed,
i'll soon forget.

but my heart
will always remember
the feeling of kinship,
the easy discourse,
the absence of walls
as we shared
common hurts and victories,
stories of love, of brokenness,
of redemption, and loss.

God ordains every encounter.
Lord, thank you for exactly who
you knew I needed,
and that she needed me, too.

MORE THAN

you are more than enough, my dear
worthy of love and compassion
treasured by your Creator

you are none of the things
your internal critic
says you are

but everything God says about you
is true

let His voice be the loudest,
His Word your guide,

and—if you do—His grace
will never let you down

HOPE

i love sleep
and peace
and restful days
when i can feel, directly, the presence of my Savior.
i love solitude
and openness
with myself;
on days when i allow Him to come in, i have found the answer
to the struggle
with loneliness—
not that I will never feel lonely,
but that hopeless
will never get the last word.

MARGINS

The best
things in
life
are often
in the
margins—
daily things—
routines—
this is
where we
are
blessed,
the call
of our
lives
answered
each day,
one at
a time,
on a
journey to
fulfill
His
purpose
for us.

LOOK AT YOU

look at you:
living and thriving,
miraculously restored,
calm and grounded,
depending on God and not people,
but loving both the lovely
and the unlovable.

look where you were,
resigned to mere survival—
now you stand ready
to answer any call,
full of health and joy
where once there was hopelessness.

that's what God does.

HIS

i still wonder at the sheer peace
i have learned to summon.

still wonder at the ability to calm
and ready myself.

regardless of circumstance,
despite all the noise,
mine is a limitless reserve of serenity.

but only because i am His,
and because He is mine.

NAMES I'VE BEEN CALLED

Maria
daughter
friend
mother
student
leader
writer
spiritual being
loved one
failure
overcomer
resilient
worthless
a dependent
a bitch
an idiot
selfish
positive
hopeful
parent

adventurer
fraud
burden
warrior
recovering addict
a waste

Call me what you want,
but my real name
is Child of God.

I KNOW

unseen flower, I see your fragrance
and I know that your petals are
drifting down on me through dewy air

invisible singer, your voice rests upon
my ear in the wind and in the rain
and in my heart's cry

blessed angel, your strength exceeds
my weakness, and your light shines
through my darkness

your love is assurance
your touch is divine
your presence is holy

and your wings are spread wide
about my shoulders, lightly touching me
and shielding me from harm

GRATEFUL

everything for a reason,
they say
but sometimes
it feels impossible

hopeless

scary

in those times
we are called
to share what God
has done for us

and as we do,
we become more and more
like Him

i never dreamed
i would become
so infinitely grateful
for the trials i have faced,

but grateful I am

RECIPE

it's the same old recipe—
½ cup of shame
a tbsp pride
a dash of self-loathing
a meal of this kind
can ravage us for days (and then some)
yet, day after day,
we make it our sustenance.

this is a habit—a cycle—we cannot break alone.
thank God, we don't have to.

WHO ARE WE?

it's not easy to forgive—
pride always comes to play
the moment our ego is bruised,
and pride renders us
powerless to extend
what we ourselves
do not deserve;
as He has forgiven us so many
more times than 7x70,
who are we to nurse our resentments
and greedily withhold
the same forgiveness
from others?

JESUS

a perfect,
breathing moment
is one
in which
a smile
lights the face,
a tear dims the eye,
and my heart
is so drenched with you
that there is no room left for me

LESSONS &
RESILIENCE

IT'S TIME

when it stops feeling like love
when it starts to hurt and then
hurts more and more

when you want to stay but
you've given all you have
and it feels like not-enough

when all you have left are
excuses you've made for their actions and
suddenly you realize THIS is the real them

it's time, love. it's time.

FLYING

he decided
I wasn't human
is the only explanation I can fathom

because no one
willingly ruins
another human
and he was more than willing
to ruin me
and in the name of God, no less

unfortunately—for him—
when he cut off my legs
he quickly learned
that I can fly

all the strongest humans can,
in truth,
which is exactly why
we are not welcome
in a world that hates
everything that is
free

HURRY

dishes calling
laundry piling
an ache to fill
tasks to complete

more focus
striving
doing
planning—willful
hurry. rush. wait. more. not enough. too much.
go
do
try
fight
act
Now.
tomorrow, no rest
next week, no time to breathe
achieve
comply
compare
reach.
earn that love—the deeply sought acceptance—the world's trophies

make a name for yourself—
but then what?
if all we do is make a name,
who will be there to call it?

TWO

There were two—them—
but also He and She;
He was lauded,
She disgraced.

Ironically, while He
suffered nothing,
and She suffered much,
today it is She who soars,
while He stands in the very same spot
where She left him.

I am so tired of watching
the injustice of a world
where incredible women
are of no value
outside of what they are willing
to give away.

LET'S LIVE

Let's look at the sky,
create music
that mirrors
the world around us

examine its darker side

embrace beauty

surround tables with mothers and fathers and all who would eat

clear heads

a deep gladness

Let's write a story of Nows,
lending something of ourselves—
wisdom—magic—

to the world's deep hunger

a knowing, a trust

quiet hearts

best lives

poured out for the joy

of living

SHE NEEDS

speak to her
encourage
ask questions
take time to understand
her highs and lows
her permanent illness
push for her to regain her independence
because you know full well
she can fight dragons single-handedly
slay a few here and there
protect her
but
hold on loosely
so she can breathe

DIFFERENT

i've always felt a little different,
the sensation of watching through glass
as other people live their very real lives.
the older i get, the more i realize
i'm not the only one;
i'm not alone.

we are all hiding behind something.

PERSONAL

I have learned
from my mistakes
and my eyes
are now wide open

there is truly
no need to seek
approval from others

no need to regret
anything from the past

because at the end of the day
this is a personal journey

HEAVY

i wish i could
share my story
without fear of judgment
but share i will,
fear be damned.

i share to quell
a burning need to be of help
to others
and because my spirit
is heavy
with all that i haven't yet
been brave enough
to lay down.

BELIEF

i get comfortable, and i slip
and suddenly
it all comes rushing back to me

the loneliness of the memories
are the hardest part
to hear and see replayed

lonely as the one i trusted
to prop me up
had cut me down instead

over and over

who do you believe
when there are so many versions of them and
they know your weaknesses
like a map of their favorite place?

who do you believe when
some say abuse and your heart says
my own fault?

i can't believe myself
and this is why:

i still don't know the truth. do you?

INVISIBLE

What do you mean, invisible?
Can you not see?
The weariness in my limbs,
the clench of a jaw, that
never gets a chance to let go—
to relax—to be soft.
The shards that pierce my
abdomen,
from the inside out,
the nervous tension of waiting
until the pain hits and
it doesn't matter any longer
about discretion, embarrassment,
or the wanting to slip through
the cracks in the floor.

Can you not see?
The body at war with the mind;
the sadness of burdening those
who never let me down, who
help me stay upright, when even
that begins to feel like
an impossible task.

The days and days and
days of symptoms, exhaustion,
anxiety over all those lost responsibilities
the failure to provide
the weight of dependency—
not to mention those
who simply are not acquainted
with constant discomfort, and who see
weakness
where in me lies more strength
than their eyes could possibly perceive.

What do you mean, invisible?
It's in every line on my face,
in every fluctuating pound,
in the carousel of pain,
nausea, and utter loss of control—
on a ride that spins at a pace that
most could never sustain.
It's in every glance,
every offhanded comment,
every accusation (both spoken and reserved)—
that I somehow enjoy this?
that I would ever choose this?
that I am less than for bearing this?

No, not invisible; not the illness.
It's there if you look
closely. It's there if you listen
to the words I DON'T say.
The illness is often the first face
I see when confronting a mirror;
Don't you see it, sitting squarely
on my chest—
on my shoulders—
trying to hold me down?

Not invisible, this illness,
but clearly written on the timeline
of my life, woven in and through
accomplishments, its weight pulling
them over, toppling each and every
triumph,
until failure is all I can
recall.

The only invisibility in this picture
of a life
is the strength that sustains it,
the courage, the rod
that runs through my spine,
vertical,

60

never giving up, but—oh, sometimes—
so much wanting to lay down
and let it all pass by.

The tenacity of a girl who wants
to be extraordinary, but
on some days cannot even
fulfill the mundane.
The ache of wanting to be seen,
understood,
validated,
valued for what I bring to life
rather than
what I simply cannot.

She may well be invisible to you;
if that is so, then the loss is yours.
She is worth every ounce of all it takes
to survive, and
She is more beautiful in the hurting
than in the relief,
for there, in the hurting,
shines a heart that will never surrender.

SINKING

underwater games, depths of frustration
all around us
eyeing you through glassy film
hearing your song through altered ears
catching only a remnant of your idea

i try but cannot understand
and as i go frantic
the water presses down on my head
and you are floated to the surface
Seeing you rise, i smile

i sink

IS IT JUST ME?

is it just me?

am i the only one who feels
she never quite
fits?

these questions—
one small doubt or misstep
and
i go right back there
right back to condemning
my life and my choices—
all the good, all the bad,
all the imagined and dreamed,
tossed out as rags

why do i descend
to this place each time,
and why can't i ever quite
seem to let go?

everyone is a warrior
we all fight, some physically,
some with the strength from our very center
battling forces for which we are no match,
some in constant struggle with self

but though we hold this in common
as our truth,
though we are all
fighting indeed,
this is where
the similarities end

our uniforms, our allegiances,
our weapons of choice
are all unique,
each of us wearing our own armor
for self-preservation

or is it only me?

FALLING

she flew
never walked
floated on assurance
trusted her voice within
believed she was whole and happy
and always would be
it hurt when she
fell
it was scary and dark
and so very lonely

she couldn't remember how she'd been okay before
but she knew she wasn't now
something was broken within her
she shattered and drifted
pushed until she snapped
and then the pills came for her

the numbness
the relief
the feeling, however fleeting, of security
the antidote for crisis
which she found she inhabited
quite frequently

so she laid down
she gave up
she let herself go

she fought but felt unworthy
even when she had prevailed
in a battle that most could not win
she deserved less
so she allowed less for herself
expected less of herself
felt ashamed of herself

she hid and then emerged
giving just enough to keep others at bay
she watched people live all around her
and she made believe

she pretended she felt like them
lived like them
had the same goals they did
--

her goal, in truth, was merely survival

but the most beautiful part of redemption
is that it is complete
it's illogical—almost magical

and she can feel it
her own redemption
can feel old parts of her
breathing their way back to life

and when she looks at you
she knows she is safe here
she knows she is loved
and so she lives

SOME DAYS

some days hurt
when my tough persona
and my faith
are shaken by a seemingly innocuous
event, word, thought
the old fears start to awaken
stretching from the long rest
and clamping cold hands
around my heart

on these days
it's all I can do to survive
to pass the time
to hope and pray they'll go
back to sleep and stay away
for good this time

not being seen or understood
for the warrior i have been
makes it difficult to
keep wearing the brave face
to keep believing and trusting and waiting
for the right time to live again

will i ever be free of these thoughts that suck me dry?

RETREAT

when I retreated to heal
someone told me I was
hiding from the world
and not living my life,
but the truth is the opposite:

previously, I was hiding IN the world
and wasting my life

NOTHING

the ache feels my head
and sweeps it up
I taste the notes of
a song above my heart
outside of my mind's reach
my clothes
wear my body
holding me up in the seat
which feels my back
the pen pulls my hand along
and the words drive my gut
I control nothing

WAIT

the girl I remember
watched the days go by
and every now and then
she lived one

her detachment protected her
from the dangerous bliss
of belonging and the horrifying chance
of embarrassment

she felt the blow of
a thousand fists in the pit of her stomach
when she witnessed
a dying love,
but she shared no love of her own

even now, guided by hopes of a future
of living, her days are spent
in glaring realization of her differences

she is an observer of life
but one day she will live

UNDONE

something comes to mind
but my mind can't comprehend it
a thought flashes by
on the brink of understanding,
but it escapes me
lying alone on my couch,
feet bare and arms clutched
around my shoulders for comfort
i stare apathetically at the screen
a million better things i could be doing
bounce around inside my guilty conscience
i ignore the nagging urges to move from my rest
and do something productive
all i want is everything,
but i cannot find the motivation to do anything at all
the fleeting thought returns,
and once again, i am suspended in
the puzzle of my life
as the pieces fall away,
purpose eludes me
scared and hollowed out,

i dream of a day when i could cry
when i could hold out arms to human contact
and accept supporting squeezes
i am unattached
unapproachable
extinct

MOST

Most would have given up—
once left alone at rehab,
once left behind by supposed friends.

Most would have quit years ago—
money all spent
and health having taken her career,
the calling she had thought was her purpose.

Most would lie down, that bone-tired,
and never get up,
never reinventing or learning to fill a new cup.

But she poured herself out,
again and again,
until she felt she was at least a shadow
of who she'd been before.

She prayed and she focused,
and systematically, she re-engaged
in a life that most
would've long since thrown away.

She squeezed glue into the seams and cracks,
and she held herself together.

Until she awoke one day and
found—felt in her soul—that
she was back.

She thought that he could see
where the light was peeking through;
though no longer shattered,
she wasn't ready for what he would do.

He didn't see her there,
didn't realize;

he pulled her apart, first a little
and then more and more as she
crawled further inside herself.

In that place where glue and
prayers
can't sustain a beating heart,
she finally laid down,
slipping back
into the safety of the darkness.

BREAK

break, break, break;
before you explode me
into extinction!
i have never felt such rage
at any human
as i do at my own heart,
which rests constantly
and perilously on the edge
of the void
between blank and shattered.

NIGHT

night has fallen
without me again
the world sleeps
and I listen to its groaning sighs

my ears—sensitive—
detecting every squeak

something draws me from sleep
holds open the door of consciousness

my future desire lies in sleep
one day, it will be an easy task
night will include me,
instead of holding me captive,
just outside its iron gates

I will fall inside
among the pillowy clouds of dream,
and I will sleep

SHAKING

endings terrify me,
and beginnings shake me, too;
anticipating the newness and dreading
the dreamt-up difficulties
leaves me reeling

hang on for today
hope for a better tomorrow

balance out the torrent

STRONGER

a voice that shakes
can still be confidently
in control
and
happy doesn't always mean smiling

PURPOSE

purpose makes
time
collapse

AFRAID

screaming at the chance
of waking up and finding
feelings changed by sunrise;
dancing with the ecstasy
of breath and hearts
and arms and gentle face—
but, bleak, dark, bitter chances
corner thoughts,
capture dreams.
your heart,
your eyes,
your words,
blissful touch,
empty breath of peace,
full sigh of contented
happy-sweet-relief.
your pain,
your smile,
your laughter,
a cry,
a tear,
an ache.

A second—a glimpse—
and night fades
into painful
darkened day.

LOST

i used to be a leader. successful. brave and strong.
the life of every party.
ambitious, proud, driven.
a bread-winner. an over-achiever.
surrounded by friends, finding belonging among them.
i used to run and work out and shatter goals with little problem.
i used to feel purposeful and important and needed;
i stood out in a crowd in a positive way.
took risks and felt much of every emotion.
i used to laugh and relax without fear of the future or fear of
failing again.
i used to win; i used to matter.
just as my body's defenses don't recognize
the parts of me they destroy,
i don't recognize this reflection,
don't know exactly who i am.
and there are very few things i fear
more than never being who i once was again.

FORGIVING

Do you know how it feels when someone tears you down?
To break into pieces and find your hero responsible for
your shattering?
You don't—won't—comprehend the shame, the confusion,
the despair.
You are not content with anything and you honor nothing.
You are a strong vessel that doesn't float—shallow, emp-
ty, pitiable.
I'll be working until the day I die at forgiving myself for you.

i

i want
i try
i believe
i can

HIDDEN FEAR

Where do happy people find their
joys
and
where do they hide their sorrows?

Someone once asked me how I am
happy
always
and I felt as empty as I ever had.

I suddenly realized
I was faced with not one
but two
great fears in my mind.

the fear I had recognized
was that some day
someone
would see my hidden pain,

and the new fear, the hidden one,
was that no one
would.

TRUST THE MESS

trust the mess
trust this lived-in house
and all the clutter

trust the couch
and the blankets
and pillows

trust the music
quietly playing
in the periphery

trust the moments of relaxation

trust yourself to get it all done,
make it all right

even if you take time to
trust, trust, trust
the mess

CHANGE

Change,
as it floats gently and tears violently through our days,
is both a dear friend and a bitter enemy.

NEED YOU

i need you
to fall apart
at the seams
on the floor
at my feet
so i can
pick you up
and laugh
you together
again
and send you
on your way

i will wait
by the door
and listen
for your shoes
on the floor
and i
will fix you up
and smile
it away again
and you
will be gone

YOU AGAIN

now is my day
to let this be your day
it's my turn to sit back and
watch you go
i won't hesitate to take a stand
when you want me to
i am strong enough, good enough
with your help

when will my resolve
become my own again?
when will i be me
without you?
how am i so caught in your strings?

let go of me
I'm going now
taking my stand
once and for all

A N E S T H E S I A

the anesthesia burning my hand,
I slipped away,
awoke to a nurse with a white styrofoam
gesture,
juice for my dry and groggy mouth.
another diagnosis,
another pill,
another day of balancing the pain of
chronic illness with
the victory of every
comfortable breath.

ALONE IN THE WATER

standing alone in the cool, blue water,
i imagined a world where i could feel nothing around me
but fluidity and waves.
the constant motion of the water and its control over my arms
and legs
and whole body reminded me of change and circumstance.
i became aware of a connection with the bugs floating on the
surface
and my companions bobbing nearby.
the afternoon sun glaring down onto my skin was enough to
drive me under
for relief from the heat.
an epiphany had come to me, and i saw the secrets of truth
in the ripples of water
always changing
but forever unchanged,
just as life, moving outward,
and outward, and outward.

ON MY WALLS

I would write truths that have
nudged their way into my consciousness,
hard-won, painful truths like
'life is not fair' and 'some things never change'
and truths that seem so obvious
but are so easy to forget—
'everything looks better in the morning' and
'this too shall pass'
I would write lyrics and fragments of poems
found and loved
My best space is one of words, words that
open my heart and make everything more clear,
more bearable
God has given us words
with which to hold one another together,
and I would write them all around me,
bandages for a weary soul.

LIVE AGAIN

I am trading in these old, stale words.
I will speak kindness and compassion over myself.
I once felt defeated by this life's trials, filled with shame and
resigned to living out my days with a sole focus on survival.
Now I am righting my course, once and for all, finding myself
fully alive, day after day.
Yes, healing is a journey.

ENDINGS

they say that true friends remain
in even the worst of times
it was a test I thought mine would ace
but some of those I counted as unconditional
fled the scene even as I was still falling

LOVE & FAMILY

MEANT

your gentle words
and tenacious loyalty
your tender ways
and relentless love

you save me every day

you love me all the way to where i'm meant to be

HEARTS

complicated hearts
feel joy to the depths
and pain at its heights

HALF

instantly completed
heart as light as air
burdens suddenly lifted
by the one
who was sent
to share the half of me
that has not yet been free to grow
the compassion to unfold
the innermost impulses
that no one can imagine
lie beneath such a
quick and tough demeanor
are now loose
untamed and changing
this defensive child
done wrong
into a woman
of courage and character
and voluntary weakness
which allows my head to bend
and my legs to give way
giving over the tense control
to be carried by the other half of you
which found its strength in me

BLUE

your eyes
are a deeper
shade of greenish-blue
every time
I look at you

your arms
feel more
like home
with each
passing day

my love
grows exponentially
every time
you show me
how much I mean to you

THE GIFT OF YOU

You'll never truly know
what you have done for me;
not only do I feel secure
in the knowledge that you love me,
but I genuinely love myself again, too.

I hadn't realized
how much I had changed myself for others
until you;
you honor my entire self,
even the silly parts,
and I am gradually becoming
the me I knew before the crash,
before the hurt, before I stopped trusting myself.

You are the something beautiful
that makes the past worthwhile.

M E

let it be me
that does that to you
let my face
end your tears
my laughter
be the life of your party
and my eyes
be the answer to
your soul-searching
questions

let it be me
that touches you

let my hands be your joy
my skin be your need
my arms be your haven of deepest rest

STAY

tremble me
with soft strong hands
grasp my heart
with your eyes
tear me gently
from my sorrows
brush away
this thin disguise

empty needs
that are not true
that necessary wants may win
come to me and stay with me
where love has never been

love me deep
as oceans rolling
touch me deep
as razor's slice
give me laughter from within
come to me and bring my life

QUIET

aching head outweighed
by comfort of nothing to do
quiet room
breeze on skin
scent of shower still lingers
sound of your voice
ringing
in
my
head
i have no idea
why i am so pleased—
i'm simply glad
you are alive
i have been given
a glimpse of what
true companionship should be
I want to hold your hands
and
look at your eyes
and your face
and your voice

WITH YOU

I like who I am when I'm with you;
you are my perfect mirror,
reflecting back to me all the best
parts of myself,
omitting all the worst.

You see me with eyes of tenderness,
with a heart ready to give,
determined to take nothing in return.

The things you like about me, the details—
the scars, the relentless will
to carry the world I've been given
on my shoulders alone—
You make me better by loving these things;
you heal me when you accept, even treasure,
what another couldn't tolerate in me,
couldn't love.

As the feelings rise within me,
my heart begins to doubt,
to fear the fall—and then I look at you,
and I see that I'm not falling alone.

Your presence assures me
that we are together in this surrender.

We don't need to fear the landing,
because you are my parachute.

And I promise you—with every touch and every glance—
that I will be yours, too.

HEALING ME

the past few years
have stretched on
and on, my life ebbing
and flowing under a
rain cloud I
could never outrun
most of the broken pieces
I managed to fashion
into something of a life,
an existence I could
sell from the outside in
hiding the pain from notice

grateful, leaning on faith alone,
I believed this was my lot,
I felt I would merely exist,
that I wasn't capable or
courageous enough to
command the kind of life I once did

building walls and retreating
into my own sanctuary of thought,
I learned the art and the power of solitude

I also learned to become paralyzed by fear,
self-preservation my full-time job

and then you. and now Us. and the walls coming down,
the lost parts of me emerging from the ruins

this life and love I never thought I deserved—
seeing me, you remind me who I am
with your touch you lift me
with your words you heal me

I'm beginning to see the sun shine again.

PRINCESS JOY

i will sit by the door
and wait for the sound
of your shoes on the floor
for your laugh, sweet
sounds, your tumbling
and dancing around

i will soak you up—,
your tiny soft face,
fairy strawberry hair,
sticky-hands-and-lips kisses—

you are my princess joy

I SEE YOU

I see you there—
a flower in the midst of
trees,
a flowing hand-made pond

a dress and sandals
a Saturday morning flea market

a song on stage
with strong, quivering
lips and hands

a house
on
a
hill

a light in the darkness
I seem to find

again
and
again

I see you there, Grandma. And I say a prayer.

REACH ME

When my spirit starts to fall
you step out of sunshine
and into my night
a whirl of madness
ever smiling
turning the corners of my mouth
upward
and speeding the flow
of blood in my veins

amidst a world where
no one can reach me
your hand stretches out
a balm for my trembling heart
touching me and pushing me
through the chaos
and teaching my heart
to love all over again

FIND ME

golden rays surround a face
a boyish smile cancels out all flaw
need for love draws me in
instead of realistic ideas
of why it is he, not I, that am off track
I tear myself down
starting at the bottom
all the way up
until I have destroyed everything
and shattered myself
I will not continue
to be the one in need
someone will find me
who has looked long and hard
and he will
look good to me
even when
he isn't
smiling

MAGIC

Bring his magic mirror,
set it up right next to my bed.
When I wake in the afternoon,
and my chest is tight,
guilt thick in my throat,
dread heavy in my head,
I will look into its ease
and drown inside the peace
of seeing me through eyes like his.

LIVE ON

my grandma lies quietly in her chair
wrapped in her fuzzy pink robe
telling stories of our childhood
my eyes scan the room
and my mind travels back
to the days of kidwashers and footstool hair-washing
over the sink
the nights of long t-shirts with andy
and mornings of
perfectly soggy microwave cinnamon toast
the story ends
and i snap back to the present
glancing at my sister
i can read on her face
that she feels just as I do
that nothing has changed
although white peach fuzz has replaced
long brown curls with tortoise-shell combs
her beauty still shines through—
whatever time has in store for us,
the love will always live

THE PLACE I LOVE MOST

At Grandma and Grandpa Gray's,
where flowers bloom
all year round—it seems—
the porch overflows with calm and beauty
baskets and trinkets adorn my mind
and troubles melt—
childhood memories ache upon me
and longing blends with smiles
the yellow bedroom may be green with ivy now
but always sunshine yellow in the corner of my mind
where stubborn happiness is kept
fairy tales are not too far to grab
when I am over the hill and far away

FRED

a wide smile—
perfectly mine alone

eyes shining with pride
and an unconditional adoration

arms soft when I need
a soft place to land
but solid and ready to protect—
at all costs—and at a moment's notice

in all of my wandering and seeking,
I never imagined that home
would be here—not in a place,
but next to you, held within
a heart true and pure,
singularly focused on
our shared present and future

my belonging is found
within the circle of your embrace
and in the heart of a God
loving enough to give me you

MOVED

they move me to tears
all of them
when they love/kiss/hug me,
I cry.
when they start to change,
when I know they are never coming back to
who they are right now,
the love,love,love and the pain/ache move me again.
All those tears are worth it—
to feel their love, watch them grow, be their Mom.

MASON GRAY

grown from the start,
you skipped right over
the baby phase—
your toddler legs
always moving
always keeping up
with your older siblings
and cousins

so responsible, so intelligent,
and such a perfect gentleman
when the need for a gentleman arises

forever putting a smile on my lips
and a laugh in my heart
with your youngest-of-the-family
silliness and quick sense of humor

always pushing the limits
but also wise to understand
that there is a time and place
for everything

I have no doubt that your future
will be dazzling;
I have every confidence in the man you'll become

I have seen glimpses of him since the day you were born

TREASURE

there is something about
a son's love, a daughter's heart—
unconditional,
uninhibited,
complete—
that keeps a mom going,
that makes it all worthwhile

they say you never stop
being a parent,
no matter the ages
your children reach

I, for one, can't imagine
a day,
couldn't fathom
a moment

of being anything less than your Mom.

SAFE

here I go again
questioning my happiness
the acme anvil girl
anticipating the worst as self-preservation

I can usually poke holes in anyone's story
so I do

but now,
everything is
upside down
and I marvel at the ways
you prove
that I am safe
with you

SELF-LOVE

she has lived through joy unbounded
and she has overcome seemingly impossible times
when all she could see was the past

she has failed, and
she has soared

she is only human, after all

she possesses in her heart
a resilient peace
where once she held on
to the wrong things and people

she has traded bravery for courage
because only courage involves the heart

she is finally learning to let go
and trust God
and she is learning to trust herself again

I am proud of her growth
she is changing in beautiful ways

she knows her worth
she is worthy of love

I love her:
she is me

YOU'RE STILL HERE

Your hair in fuzzy yellow curlers, you picked me up from school
the day my period sent me fleeing from class.
Then, embarrassed, I feared someone would see you.

Today, I would give almost anything
to show you to my three almost-adults,
to share you with the one
who holds my heart so gently.

Undeterred, you stopped for nothing, not even pain.
You planted and reaped,
providing gorgeous food for our family.

You cooked effortlessly and on a moment's notice,
as you did on my 1st wedding day,
wowing my bridesmaids and calming my jitters—
you there serving and Grandpa entertaining, as always.

Your place in Florida,
your Nuisance of an alligator,
bingo in the activity hall--
I can see it all so clearly in my mind,
and oh-what-i-would-do
to be there with you again.

You believed in my dreams always,
as so perfectly evidenced by
my shiny, new library card and
subscription to REAL teacher magazines.

You were so strong, and you were steady.
You didn't profess love
in an open, physical way,
but you loved.
You loved through action; you loved completely.

I knew.
You gave me that gift without words.

I see so much of You in my mom,
and I see so very much of her in me.
Smiling, I realize this means that you are still here,
carried in the hearts of those of us
privileged to have known your love.

ALWAYS

i will always be
healing but broken
afraid but courageous
even more
i will always love you

TO MY SON, EJ

Your little boy legs
running next to mine
and then, in a blink,
you are grown.

Your legs now carry you
away, each step bringing
closer the day
when you are no longer here with me.

Flashes of memory alight in my mind,
a movie reel of moments,
which add up to a whole life—
the life of my firstborn.

Egg dripping down from your head;
your feet pounding up the stairs
and racing to the door to collect
your gummy pizza delivery;
squealing and shivering through the backyard
as I spray you with the water hose;
your face lit up by a birthday candle;
a scene from your annual Christmas show at Kathy's

your smile as you arrive on the bus from the elementary to the
high school
where I am the principal.

I see you flying your whale balloon,
riding through the halls of my newest school on your hoverboard,
happily singing with your classmates for Mother's Day at
Guiding Hands Preschool,
accepting Jesus as your Lord and Savior.

I waited for you through over a month
of hospital bed rest,
and you were SO worth the wait.

Ironically, I have continued to wait
for your next move through the years
as you have grown and developed
at your own pace.

An example: You weren't yet putting words together
at almost 3, and the doctor wanted
to place you in First Steps, but I knew
you were waiting until you could speak confidently.
And speak you did, not long after that appointment
and in complete sentences.

With each ACE Award you won in middle school,
your teachers spoke of how quiet you were
until suddenly you were helping others in the class,
opening up and learning with enthusiasm.

You've always done things when you were ready,
so I have learned to let you have that space,
and you have never disappointed.
You always find your way.

From the boy who loved to line up his toys in a parade of sorts,
who asked for the most random Christmas gifts
and usually at very short notice,
you've become a young man,
one who has put in the work
to earn admission and scholarships to Indiana State at no cost,
for the first year at least. Be proud. I certainly am.

The past few years have held some tough moments.
I've been sick a lot, and we have moved several times;
we struggled financially with my inability to work for
a two-year period;
we lost family we thought were forever.

Through all of this, you have never complained,
you have shown compassion for my illness,
and you have (along with your siblings)
been my motivation to keep getting up again.

That's exactly what I hope for you.
I hope you pursue what makes you happy
and never give up, even when life is unkind.
I hope and I pray—for your safety,
for your future, for your happiness and health.
I will pray this over you every day,
as long as I'm alive.

There aren't adequate words
to convey how much I love you
or how proud I am to be your mom.
Life will challenge you, but know that when it does,
I will be right here;
between me and God, you will never be alone.

PRICELESS

you say failure
but I say diligence, provision, ruthless protection

you say letting us down
but you only lift me up, time and time again

you see accounts and balances and the way
our pasts depleted our resources,
but you forget that while I was once shattered and empty,
you brought healing
and filled my life and my heart
with all I could truly need
apart from God

I prayed for relief from the numb resignation
that I was done—
done being the woman I recognized
and wanted to be,
done trying to grasp old dreams
that had come to seem foolish,
hopeless, and vain

the riches you brought to my door and my life
that October evening—
those are what I see

what you have gifted to me—what you have brought—
is utterly priceless

AMELIA

I wish I had the words
to ensure you'd always know
how very proud I am
of the young woman you've become

if anything
I shake my head in wonder
that a person so strong, talented, and self-possessed
could have come, even in half, from me

so much of what you do
fear would never have allowed for me
and I regularly stand in awe
of your courage

there will never be a day in this life
that you will go unloved,
for whatever is in store for me,
and however late or soon I leave this world

the love I have for you will remain

NEVER

I have never felt quite this way
this butterflies-in-the-stomach
excitement
coupled with security
and a deep sense of contentment

I have never felt I mattered
I felt loved for all the wrong reasons—
for what I could bring to the table

there are a million more "I never"s we have shared
and a lifetime more to come

for today my favorite is this:
until you,
I had never truly believed in forever

REAL

you aren't an antidote
for all my aches or suffering
no, you cannot heal
all that ails me
inside or out

but your presence
makes me strong enough
to heal and anchor my heart

your kindness gives me courage
enough to grow and challenge
who I am

and your adoration, your devotion, your love—
they help me love myself again

FINAL NOTE

I have been afraid of change as long as I can remember.

A risk taker at heart, I fling myself at each new opportunity I encounter, and much more often than not, I succeed. To the outside world, I am bold and strong—not afraid of much. Put me in an airplane, and I'll jump out of it. Put me in a crowd, and I'll entertain every person in it.

The truth is I've been living terrified almost my entire life. My dad and I joke that we are "acme anvil people", waiting for the next big hunk of metal to fall out of the sky and take away our joy. While outwardly diving headlong into every endeavor, I have lived as long as I can remember with an almost debilitating need to control.

Control my job. Control my future. Control my relationships. Control my emotions. Control today, control tomorrow, and the next day, and the next day, and the next.

I have accomplished much in my years. With precision and force, I have wrangled life into what I want it to be. But all that pleasing and succeeding can come with a price. Too many moments of peace and happiness and actually enjoying the gifts around me have been wasted in worrying about what might be lost or missed if I didn't try—or work, or push, or hold on—hard enough.

The events of the past few years of my life have been utterly beyond my power to control. I have made wrong turns, taken leaps of faith, and been handed more than my share of "bad luck", or so it seems at times.

Somewhere along the way, I made a decision. I decided to stop working to please others and take a chance at a kind of happiness that has nothing to do with the outside world and everything to do with being true to myself.

Why tell this story? Because I have a message. A message for anyone living in fear like I was.

I've failed. I've fallen. For the first time in my stubborn-as-any-mule history, I have had to ask for help. A lot. And some of my worst fears came true. But, you know what? Most of them didn't. And the ones that did? They didn't kill me. And there have been blessings I couldn't have dreamed for myself and wouldn't have dared to imagine.

When the shit hit the fan, and the rubber met the road, many of the people I had trusted most let me down (because they are only human, after all), but most of them didn't. More of the good stuff presented itself, and became more noticeable, and had more capacity to break down my walls and bring me, finally, to a sweet happiness.

Were my worries and fears valid? Certainly. Did some of them come true? You bet they did. And there were moments of lying fetal in the bathroom floor, thinking I might never rise again. But rise again I did, and always to the realization that change really is okay. Change is beautiful and can bring redemption. Change is worth the risk.

After living in fear these many years, I now fear very little. I fear only FEAR ITSELF. Fear is the only warrior I can't defeat; if I let it into my life, it robs my joy and steals my peace.

So what am I going to do about it? I am going to tackle each day with the same confidence, fervor, and passion I have lovingly brought to my former days, but I am also going to fall into a safety net of grace that casts out any need for fear. So what if I fall? I've already proven I can fly. So what if I get kicked down? I've yet to lack the drive to get back up.

I will fear only fear itself, from this day forward, and I will deliberately throw off worry when it begins to descend upon me. I will embrace change and love my life and give generously to those around me. Will I fail? You betcha. But I'm not scared of that.

Milton Keynes UK
Ingram Content Group UK Ltd.
UKHW040644041023
429927UK00004B/255